ARABIC PATTERNS
COLORING BOOK

J. BOURGOIN

DOVER PUBLICATIONS, INC.
MINEOLA, NEW YORK

NOTE

Unlike Western art, which abounds with images of the human figure and landscapes, traditional Arabic art, under the influence of Islam, is based on elaborate geometric patterns and linear designs. Its main object is not to convey a deep personal feeling, but to elicit an appreciation for details. The art in this collection is based on renderings by the French art historian J. Bourgoin in a rare late-nineteenth century pictorial album. Each of the thirty-one full page patterns is perfect for experimentation with color, plus, perforated pages make displaying your work easy.

Bibliographical Note

Arabic Patterns Coloring Book, published by Dover Publications, Inc., in 2013, is a republication of a selection of plates from *Arabic Allover Patterns,* originally published by Dover in 1985.

International Standard Book Number

ISBN-13: 978-0-486-49486-9
ISBN-10: 0-486-49486-1

Manufactured in the United States by Courier Corporation
49486101   2013
www.doverpublications.com

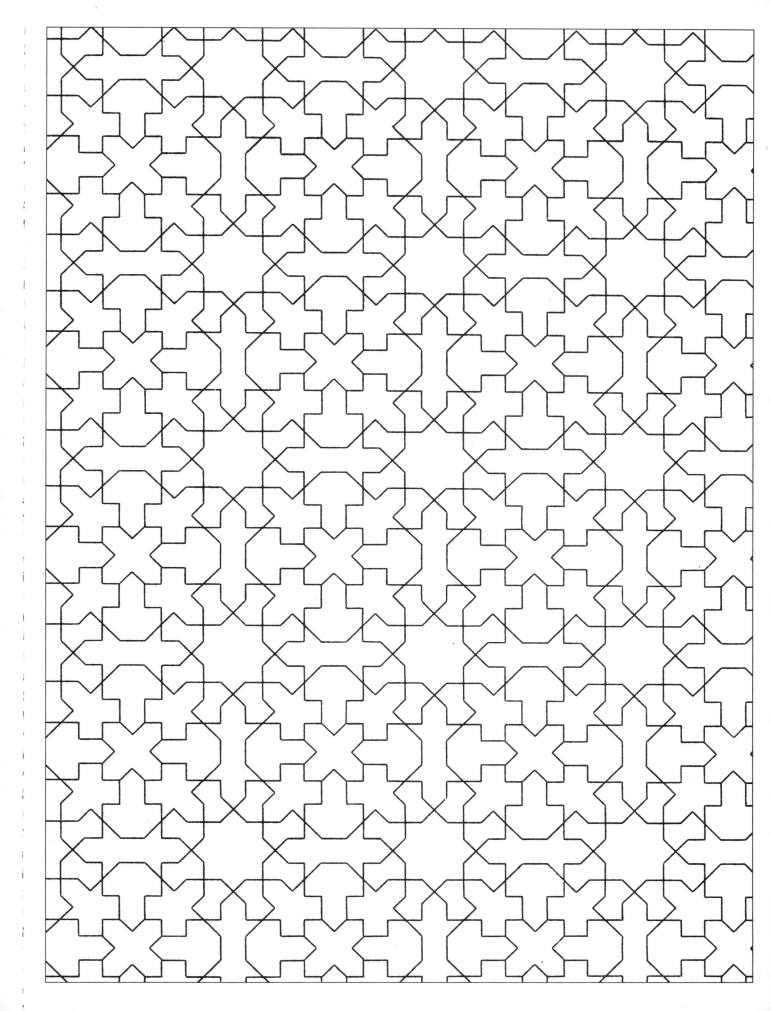

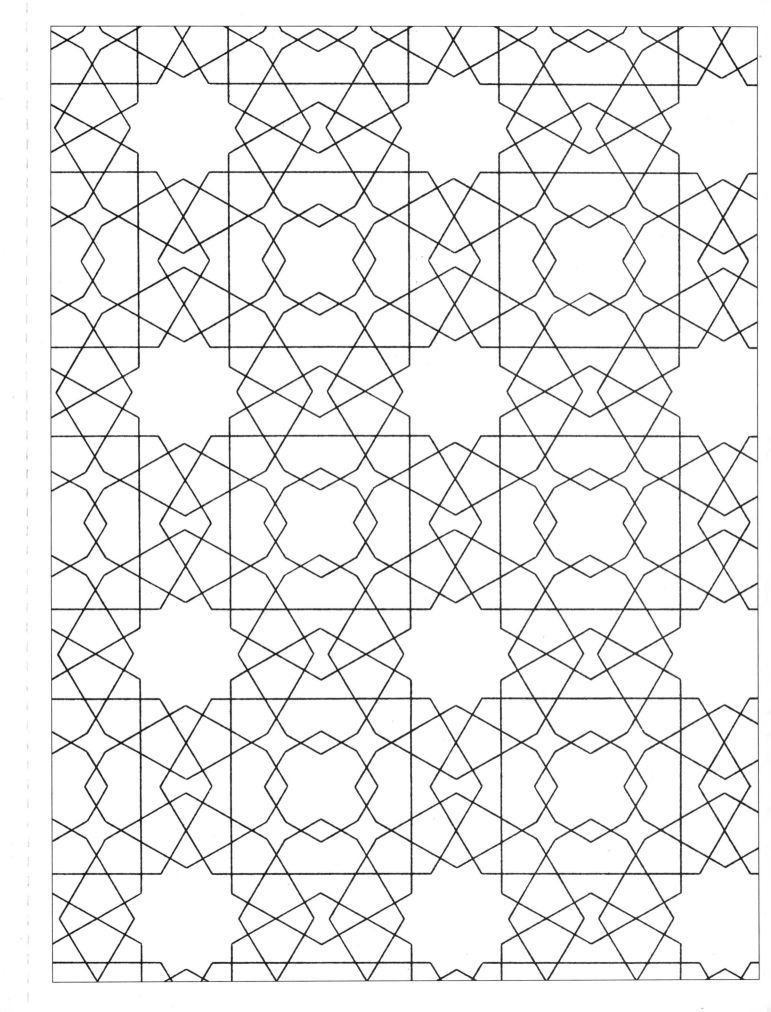

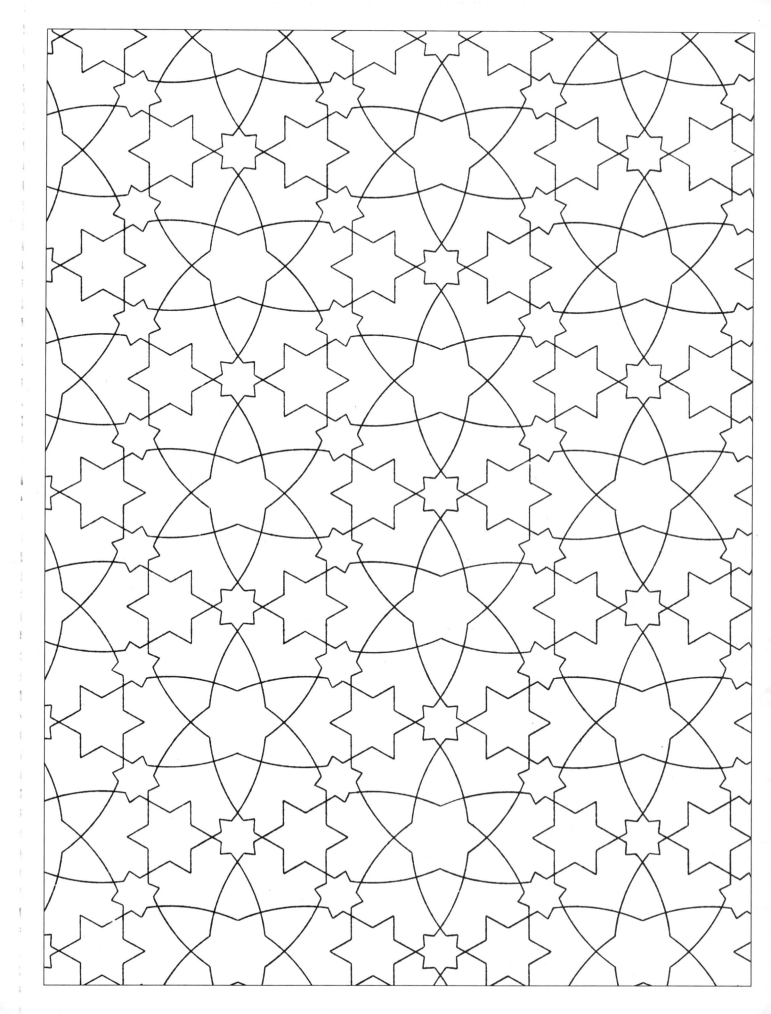